THE MOVIE GUIDE

LONDON, NEW YORK, MELBOURNE,
MUNICH, AND DELHI

PROJECT EDITOR Heather Scott

PUBLISHING MANAGER Simon Beecroft

SENIOR DESIGNER Nathan Martin

BRAND MANAGER Robert Perry

DTP DESIGNER Hanna Ländin

CATEGORY PUBLISHER Alex Allan/Siobhan Williamson

PRODUCTION CONTROLLER Vivianne Ridgeway

First published in the United States in 2007 by
DK Publishing
375 Hudson Street
New York, New York 10014

07 08 09 10 11 10 9 8 7 6 5 4 3 2 1
TD257—04/07

DK books are available at special discounts when purchased in bulk for sales promotions,
premiums, fund-raising, or educational use. For details, contact:
DK Publishing Special Markets, 375 Hudson Street, New York, New York 10014
SpecialSales@dk.com

A catalog record for this book is
available from the Library of Congress.

ISBN: 978-0-7566-3013-3

Hi-res workflow proofed by Wyndeham Icon Limited, UK
Design & digital artworking by Nathan Martin
Printed and bound by Hung Hing, China

Discover more at
www.dk.com

TRANS FORMERS
THE MOVIE GUIDE

BY SIMON FURMAN

CONTENTS

Introduction 6

The Allspark: Order or Chaos? 8

Optimus Prime: Introduction 10

Optimus Prime: Robot Mode 12

Optimus Prime: Vehicle Mode 14

Optimus Prime: Weapon Mode 16

Megatron: Introduction 18

Megatron: Robot Mode 20

Megatron: Vehicle Mode 22

Megatron: Weapon Mode 24

Trans-scanning: Local Camouflage 26

Bumblebee: Introduction 28

Bumblebee: Robot Mode 30

Bumblebee: Vehicle Mode 32

Bumblebee: Weapon Mode 34

Barricade: Introduction 36

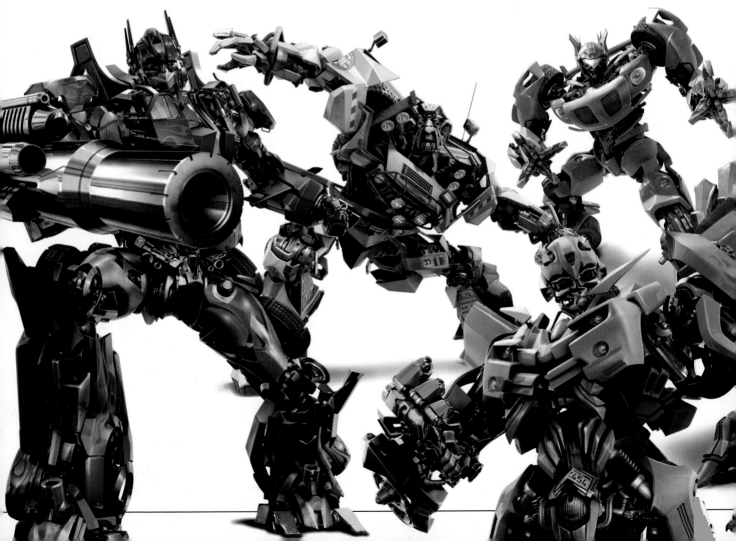

Barricade: Robot Mode   **38**

Barricade: Vehicle Mode   **40**

Barricade: Weapon Mode   **42**

Frenzy: Robot Mode   **44**

Blackout: Introduction   **46**

Blackout: Robot Mode   **48**

Blackout: Vehicle Mode   **50**

Blackout: Weapon Mode   **52**

Scorponok: Robot Mode   **54**

Jazz: Introduction   **56**

Jazz: Robot Mode   **58**

Jazz: Vehicle Mode   **60**

Jazz: Weapon Mode   **62**

Ratchet: Introduction   **64**

Ratchet: Robot Mode   **66**

Ratchet: Vehicle Mode   **68**

Ratchet: Weapon Mode   **70**

Acknowledgments   **72**

TRODUCTION

NUS PRIME

"**OUR PLANET, CYBERTRON, WAS** destroyed by the ravages of war, a war waged between the legions who worship chaos and those of us who follow freedom. We battled for control of a supreme power—the Allspark. Its origin is unknown to us, yet it bears the life force that created our race. We fought until our world was awash with death, until the very ground swallowed whole our once mighty cities and the Allspark was lost to the limitless stars. By fortune or fate, its course was altered, drawn to a planet called Earth. Every thousand solar years, the Allspark calls to us, bearing the promise of returning life to our home. We have searched for it across the deserts of time, hoping to find it before the dark legions. But, as fate would have it... we were already too late!"

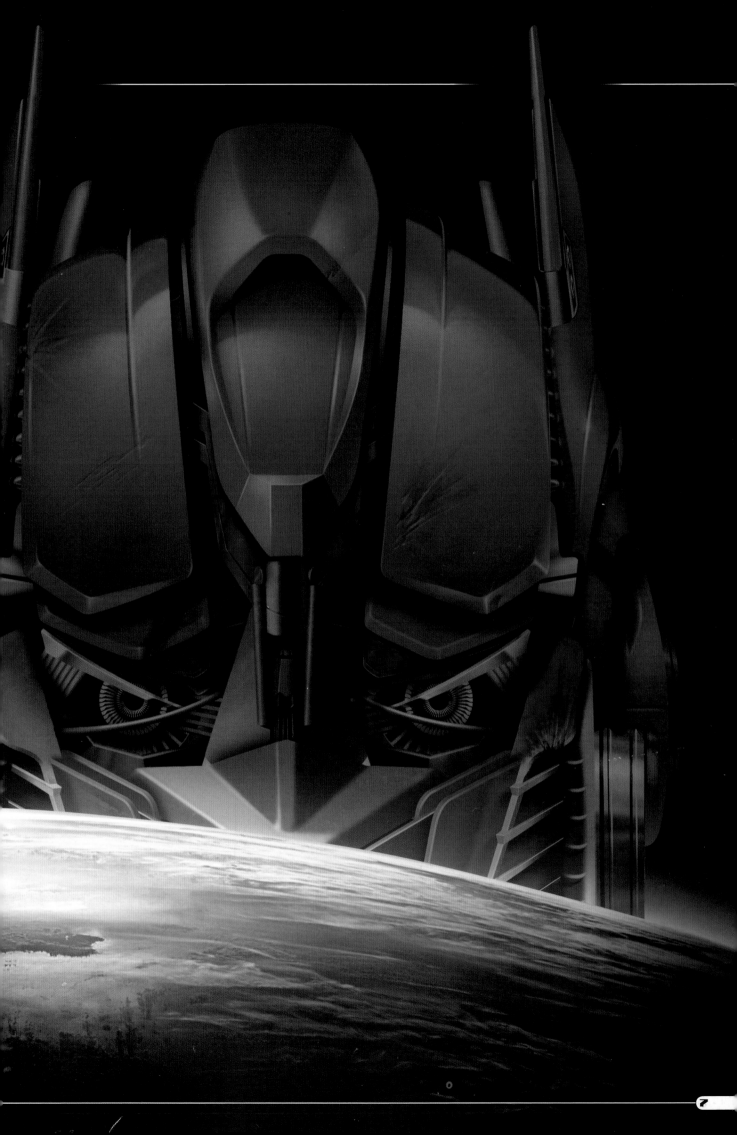

THE ALLSPARK

THE ORIGINS OF THE Allspark are lost in the mists of time and its cosmic secrets remain locked within its flawless geometry. As the ultimate source of power in the known universe, it has the ability to create or destroy. The Allspark regulated the vast currents deep beneath the surface of Cybertron, and the planet thrived and prospered. There was no strife, no inequity, and no need for war. Until, that is, Cybertron's Lord High Protector, Megatron, sought to claim the Allspark for his own twisted purposes. He plunged Cybertron into civil war and all that stood between Megatron and ultimate power was Optimus Prime.

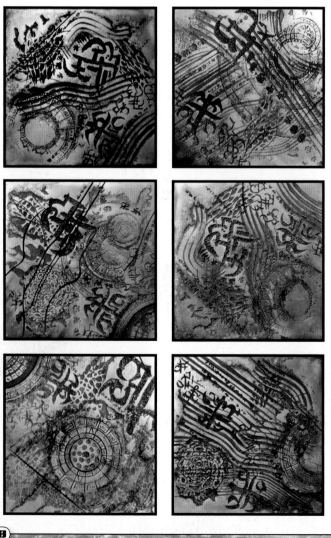

COSMIC CODE

Although no Cybertronian has ever dared to probe the inner mysteries of the Allspark, the strange alien symbols that cover its entire outer surface have been the subject of much conjecture and analysis. The most pre-eminent minds on Cybertron have wrestled with their significance, desperate to understand more about this remarkable source of life-giving energies. But, to date, no one has managed to crack this cosmic code.

Though it appears vast, the Allspark can decrease and increase its size according to circumstances.

EARTHBOUND

When it became inevitable that the hastily marshalled Autobot forces could not withstand the advance of the marauding Decepticons, Optimus Prime denied Megatron ultimate victory by launching the Allspark into the vastness of outer space. Much later, through some cosmic quirk of fate, its trajectory was altered, sending it hurtling towards planet Earth.

"FREEDOM IS THE RIGHT OF ALL SENTIENT BEINGS, WE WILL NEVER HARM HUMANS"

OPTIMUS PRIME

ROBOT MODE

A WISE AND BENEFICENT leader turned reluctant warrior hero, Optimus Prime spearheads the struggle to protect—at any cost—the sacred Allspark from Megatron's vile ambition and the corruption that seems destined to follow. In peacetime, Prime was a stoic, dignified head of state, ruling with compassion and forbearance. In wartime, despite the heavy toll of countless battles and ever-mounting casualties, those qualities still define his character.

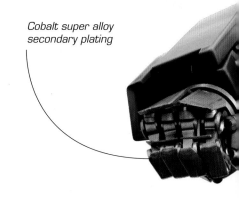

Cobalt super alloy secondary plating

FACT BOX
Optimus Prime is incredibly strong, his hyper-coil musculature gives him extreme power. However, he rarely uses his full might, fearful of collateral damage.

Gyro-balance mechanism

Height: 28'
Weight: 4.3 metric tons
Strength: Power Level 5
Vehicle: Semi-truck

Foot clamp/ locking mechanism

THE GIFT OF LIFE
"Where there is life, there is hope." So said Optimus Prime as he made desperate, last-ditch preparations to launch the Allspark into space. Prime knew full well that without the Allspark Cybertron itself might die. But, somewhere in the vast universe, the Allspark would bring its gift of life to others. For Prime, that was enough.

Core vent system

Main Spark

Hyper-coil musculature

Impact-absorption system (part)

External trim deco (chameleon mesh)

Data access port

Magnetic field generator

VEHICLE MODE

WHEN IT BECAME APPARENT that Megatron was prepared to pursue the Allspark to the very ends of the universe, Optimus Prime had no option but to search for the very thing he had tried so hard to lose in the vastness of outer space. Using the Allspark's last known trajectory as a guide, Prime and his most trusted warriors struck out for distant systems and remote stars, exploring countless planets. Finally, the trail led to Earth and an urgent summons from Bumblebee.

SYMBOLIC
Optimus Prime appreciates the need for stealth and adopts a suitable Earth-based disguise on his arrival on Earth, but his Autobot insignia is always front and centre. More than a symbol, it stands for the key Autobot principles of truth, justice, and liberty for all.

MADE TO MEASURE
Though in theory Cybertronian technology allows for the trans-scanning process to work on any given specification, in truth each robot needs a non-sentient template of roughly the same overall mass. So, when a semi-truck thundered along a nearby highway, Prime had no hesitation in reformatting his body accordingly.

FACT BOX
Optimus Prime can access extra (reserve) power from compacted energy cells on either flank. These volatile, shielded units are accessed only in emergencies.

Autobot insignia

Coolant accelerator mesh

Inter-module uplink transmitters (x2)

FACT BOX
Optimus Prime is built for sheer, unrelenting endurance rather than simply speed. His unique slow-burn engine continually recycles expended fuel.

Forward artillery muzzles

Combustion
discharge vents

Reinforced front
shielding

Surface-to-air
missile launchers

Rear targeting
scope

Chassis detailing

Rear bulletproof
tire guards

Top Speed: 250mph

0-60 in: 1.25 seconds

Engine: 850 HP

Max haulage: 600 metric tons

Traction tires

OPTIMUS PRIME

WEAPON MODE

LOCK AND LOAD

Though, more often that not, Optimus Prime would rather think or reason his way out of a tight spot, that doesn't mean he can't fight fire with fire should the circumstances so dictate. His laser-sighted barrage cannon fires plutonium-tipped warheads up to a range of 60 miles, the explosive force equal to (approx) 3000 lbs of TNT. An auto-reloader and reserve battery allow for "spread" firing. Secondary pulse weapons rapid-fire charged (10 megawatt) energy particles, creating a "firewall" effect.

Prime's leg mechanism locks when in weapon mode, providing a vibration-free firing sequence.

"CLEVER INSECT. GIVE ME THE ALLSPARK."

MEGATRON

MEGATRON

ROBOT MODE

THE FORMER LORD HIGH Protector of Cybertron, Megatron's ambitions overpowered his once firm but fair nature. In secret, he coveted the Allspark's limitless power for himself, and when he had the chance, he struck, brutally and mercilessly, his army swiftly mastering the ways of war. Consumed by sheer lust for power, Megatron soon graduated to greater atrocities, devastating the planet he once served.

THE QUEST

On Cybertron, Megatron came close to securing the Allspark. Determined to possess its life-giving powers, he homed in on the Allspark's unique energy signal. But, when the Allspark was subsequently ejected into space, he was forced to begin his quest anew.

FACT BOX
Megatron can self-repair most damage sustained to his internal systems or external armature, almost instantaneously. He is very hard to injure, let alone render inactive.

Tri-axis joint (for multifunction hand)

Probe/pincer, razor-tipped

Height: 35'
Weight: 5.7 metric tons
Strength: Power Level 5
Vehicle: Interstellar jet

Mass dispersal brace (one of four)

*Antennae, cranial
superstructure*

*Vocal interface/
sonic amplifier*

*Pincer lock/release
mechanism*

*Internal servo-
musculature*

*Blast/fragmentation
shield*

*12" cobalt/tungsten
armature*

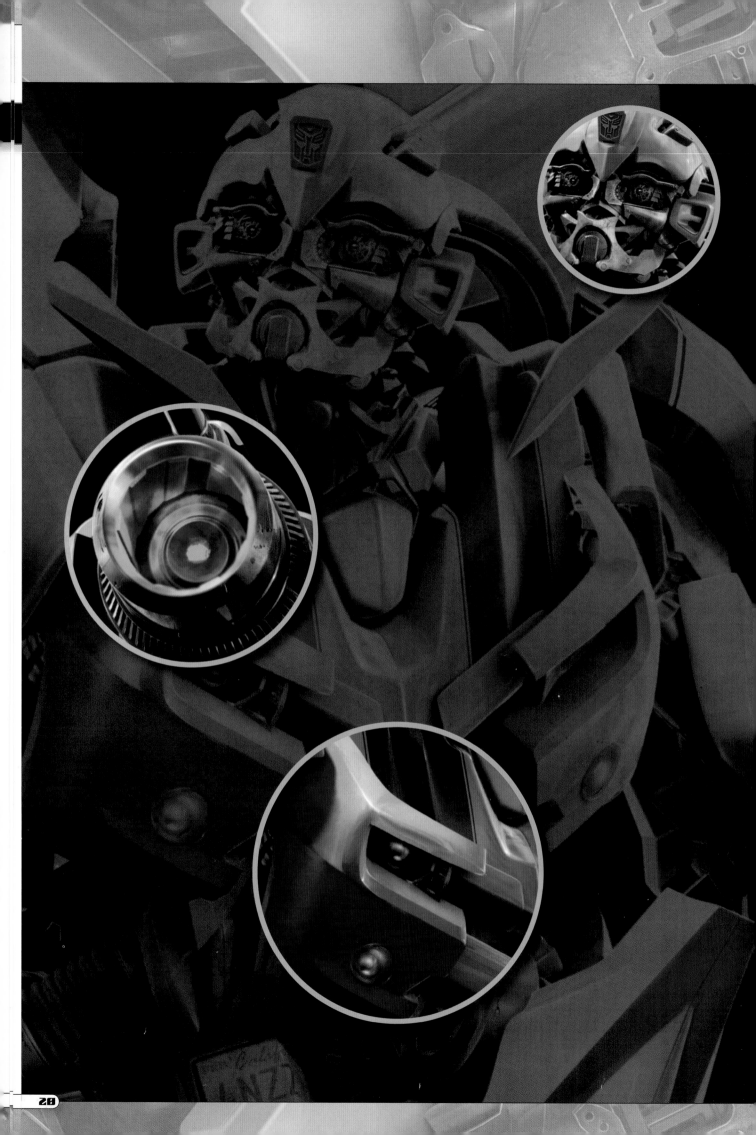

"WHO'S GONNA DRIVE YOU HOME?"

BUMBLEBEE

BUMBLEBEE

A STRONG AND ABIDING sense of duty guides and directs the actions of this tenacious and resourceful Autobot. Bumblebee doesn't want glory or accolades, he just needs to know he got the job done and done well. Sometimes, though, following orders to the letter conflicts with Bumblebee's deep well of compassion. In his capacity as a tactical ops unit leader, Bumblebee deeply regrets any loss of life, even if it is for the "greater good."

SILENT PROTECTOR

In the pivotal Cybertronian battle of Tyger Pax, Bumblebee figures large. It was he who, with the precious Allspark within Megatron's grasp, threw himself into a battle he couldn't possibly win. The critical injuries already sustained were compounded when Megatron crushed Bumblebee's vocal processor, rendering him mute.

Solar
accelerator
particle weapon

Laser targeting
sub-system

Turbo-hydraulic
musculature

FACT BOX
Bumblebee's exo-armor is coated with solar receptors and channel energy from the sun into power cells, which fuel his solar accelerator weapon.

Mass-offset system
(stealth feature)

Height: 16' 2"
Weight: 1.6 metric tons
Strength: Power Level 2
Vehicle: Chevy Camaro GTO

Tri-tanium toecap

Rear-suspension
shock buffer

Comm. receivers/
transmitters

FACT BOX
Bumblebee is comparatively
small, with less overall body
mass. However, this makes
him both fast and
maneuverable in robot mode,
and a difficult target to hit.

Solar energy receptors
(microscopic)

FACT BOX
Bumblebee can
focus his internal
power reserves into
one super-surge
attack, virtually
doubling the sheer
concussive force at
his disposal.
However, it leaves
him vulnerable.

Impact/shock
absorber

Secondary
unlink access
port

Tri-tanium fingertips
(friction-resistant)

ON THE RIGHT TRACK
Bumblebee was one of the first
TRANSFORMERS to reach Earth, having
diligently and unerringly tracked the
Allspark across the vast cosmos.
Immediately, he began to scan the
Internet, zeroing in on the story of Captain
Archibald Witwicky and the discovery of a
giant under the ice. This in turn steered
Bumblebee to Tranquility and Captain
Witwicky's great, great-grandson, Sam.

NEVER ONE TO STAND out in a crowd, Bumblebee's sheer lack of vanity meant that when selecting an Earth disguise he never even stopped to consider there might be better, newer options. The beaten-up classic Camaro he trans-scanned seemed altogether adequate for the job, and Bumblebee took its limitations in his stride. As it turned out, the selection proved ideal, as it gave Bumblebee the perfect cover in Bobby Bolivia's used car lot.

IMPRESSIVE WHEELS

The object of Sam's affections, Mikaela Banes is a fellow student at Tranquility High. Wilful, forthright (but with a dark family secret), Mikaela was a large part of the reason Sam wanted a car in the first place. Wanting to impress her, Sam managed to put her in extreme danger instead.

BUYING BUMBLEBEE

Whether Bumblebee actually meant for Sam to buy him from Bobby Bolivia's auto resale emporium, or whether he was simply observing from the best possible vantage point, we may never know (and Bumblebee's not telling!) Whatever the case, it was the right place, right time, and for Sam it was the beginning of the great adventure he'd always sought.

Bumblebee's second Earthly incarnation is a million miles away from his first: a beaten up classic Camaro.

FACT BOX
Bumblebee specializes in hit and run tactics, using his evasive skills to get in range and then his extensive in-built artillery (concussive "flash" shells) to fell his target.

Coolant accelerator fan/main intake

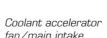

FACT BOX
Bumblebee is highly maneuverable. His traction, even in the wet, is second to none and he can zig-zag rapidly on the straight without loss of speed.

Range-finder sensor web

THE UPGRADE

When Mikaela, rather pointedly, asked why Bumblebee had chosen such a down-market disguise, the response was immediate and demonstrative. Trans-scanning a passing, just-out-of-the-showroom Concept Camaro, Bumblebee gave himself a dramatic upgrade, and gave Sam the "wheels" of his dreams. Suddenly, there were no limits to what they could do!

Top speed: 230mph

0-60 in: 0.96 seconds

Engine: 450 HP

Max haulage: 50 metric tons

Main armaments cover

Solar energy emitters (microscopic)

Stealth glass

Rear-view targeting sights

FACT BOX
Bumblebee's solar receptors can be turned into emitters in vehicle mode, generating a burst of sensor-overloading light that can render surveillance cameras useless.

Trans-scanning image intensifier

Hypertension wheel supports

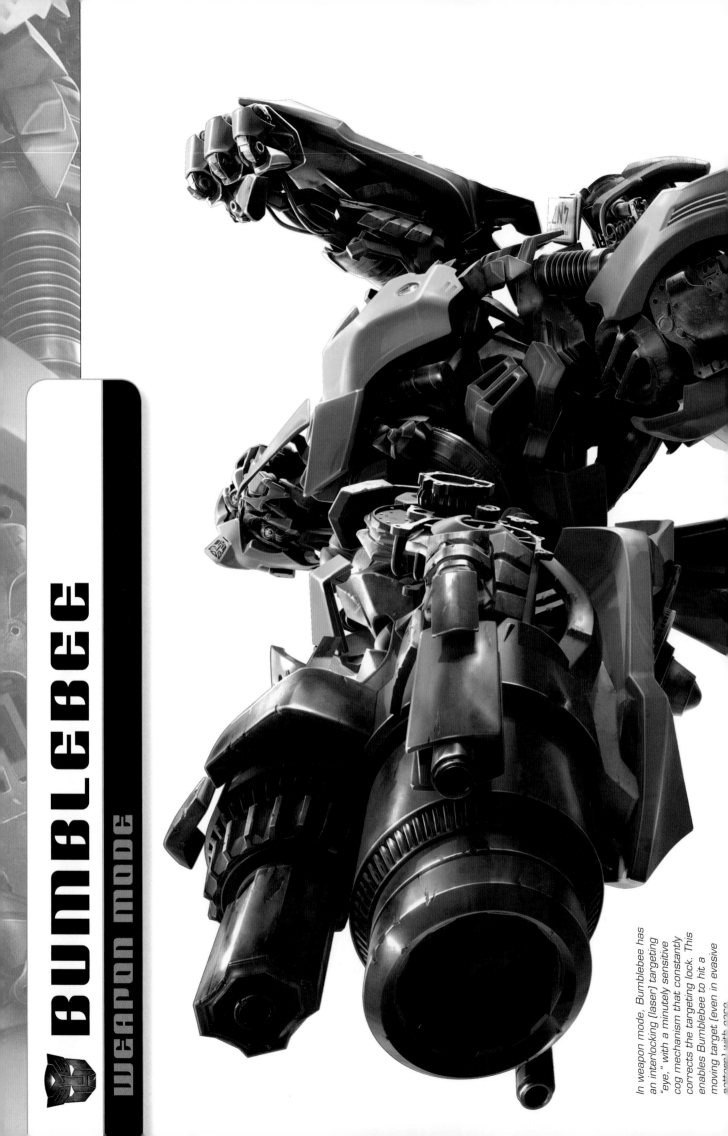

BUMBLEBEE

WEAPON MODE

In weapon mode, Bumblebee has an interlocking (laser) targeting "eye," with a minutely sensitive cog mechanism that constantly corrects the targeting lock. This enables Bumblebee to hit a moving target (even in evasive action) with ease.

STING LIKE A BEE

Bumblebee's solar accelerator/agitator weapon is one of the most lightweight and adaptable weapons ever developed for combat. Its lack of fissionable core or power cell cluster and its ultralite alloy construction means it weighs in at a mere 400 kilograms, but packs a punch equivalent to much larger weaponry. Solar energy is absorbed through Bumblebee's dermal tissue and channeled via a network of gas-filled tubes to a particle cyclotron inside the weapon itself. Agitated light is then released as a solid burst of pure concussive force, equivalent to 500 psi (at maximum output). The impact is enough to knock even Devastator off his feet, and leaves a raw, sensitive blast spot due to the abrasive nature of the supercharged particles.

"FOR NOW, WE MUST REMAIN IN DISGUISE"

BARRICADE

"SIR—SAYS HERE AF4 WAS SHOT DOWN THREE MONTHS AGO"

OP CENTER TECH

"MY FIRST LIEUTENANT. DESIGNATION: JAZZ"

OPTIMUS PRIME

WHATEVER YOU NEED, NO matter where in the world or the universe you are, Jazz can get it for you. His innate understanding of environments, alien or otherwise, and his sheer adaptability make him indispensable on any mission. Jazz absorbs information like a sponge, assimilating languages, culture, and geo-political data at breathtaking speed. Endlessly fascinated by new cultures, Jazz wants in on any kind of exploration mission.

FIRST AMONG EQUALS

Amazingly cool under pressure, Jazz proved his worth to Optimus Prime on the battlefields of Cybertron many times over. Able to process raw data and output focused, tactical info-feeds in a matter of nano-kliks, Jazz became essential as the battle for Cybertron intensified, and he was soon promoted to First Lieutenant, effectively Optimus Prime's right-hand 'bot.

Height: 15' 7"
Weight: 1.8 metric tons
Strength: Power Level 2
Vehicle: Pontiac Solstice

Intra-musculature (section)

Temperature variance meters

FACT BOX
Jazz can access a microfine sensor net, its receptors built into practically every external surface. These analyze atmospheric and environmental conditions.

Primary sensor node

FACT BOX
Jazz's visor allows him to view his environment in a wide variety of fields of vision, including thermal, infrared, X-Ray, and microscopic. Nothing escapes his attention.

FACT BOX
Jazz is very fast, in both robot and vehicular mode. His armor plating has a friction retardant surface, allowing him to almost glide through wind currents.

Friction retardant surface
Ultra-vision visor
Main uplink transmitter/ receiver
Limpet claw grip
Primary impact suppressors
Torque (leg) joint
Mag-light (unidirectional emitter)
Tri-integral support (locked)
Air filter/ analysis unit

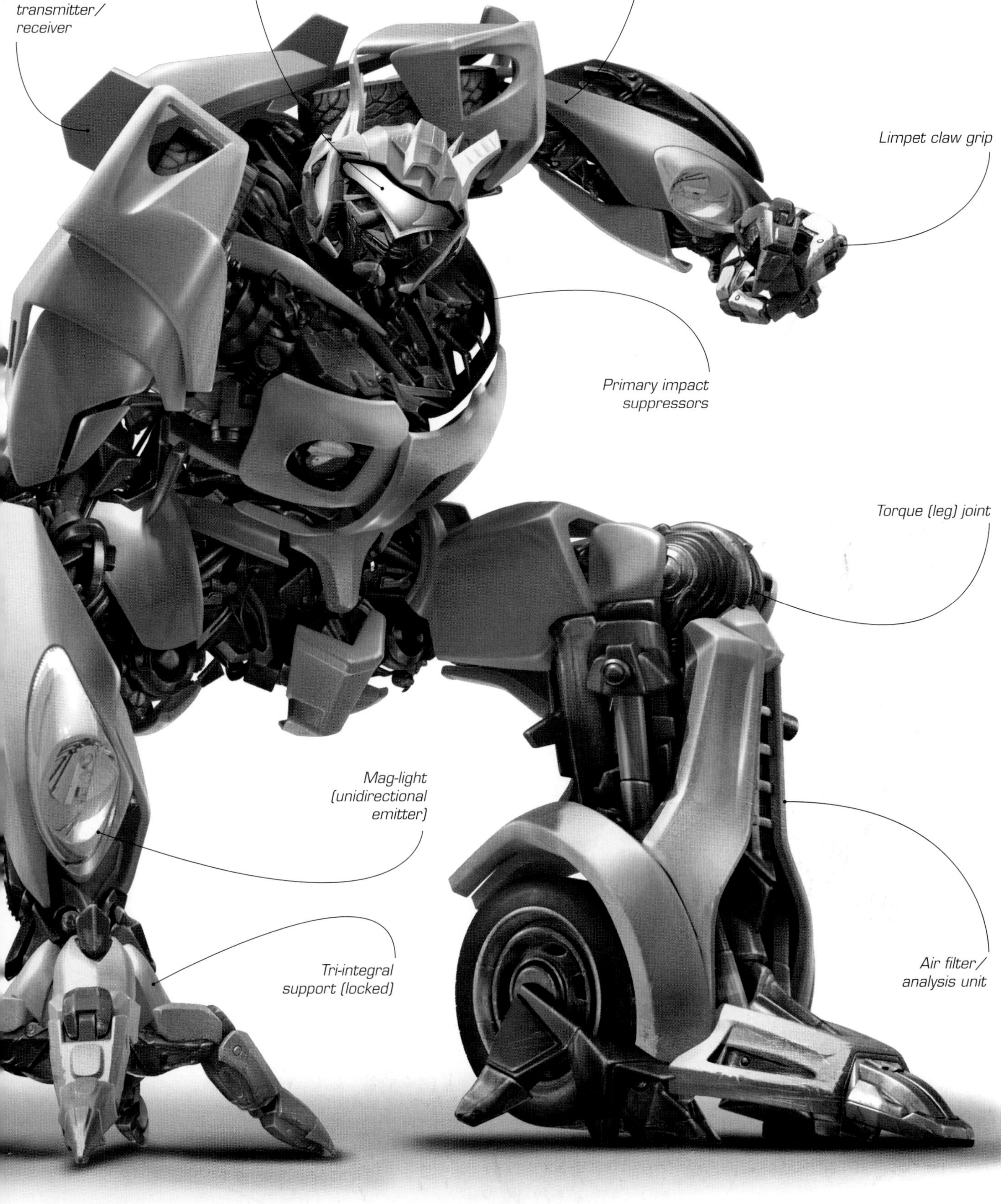

JAZZ

VEHICLE MODE

IT CAME AS LITTLE surprise to anyone that, when selecting a suitable Earth disguise, Jazz opted for something fast, sporty, and utterly eye-catching. The Pontiac Solstice suited him down to the ground, Jazz innately understanding the difference between merely functional and plain cool! The other Autobots simply opted for the first vehicle (of comparable size and mass) they clapped optics on, whereas Jazz (attuned instantly to all manner of media) set his sights just a little higher.

FACT BOX
Jazz can simultaneously receive visual and audio feed from 600 dedicated wavelengths, instantly decoding or unscrambling top-secret communiqués.

Rear-view targeting sights

Trans-scanning image intensifier

Armaments cache

Audio filter

Retractable load bearing arms

Thermal imagers

Top speed: 400mph
0-60 in: 1.07 seconds
Engine: 450 HP
Max haulage: 30 metric tons

Friction retardant
surface

Main antenna/receptor

FACT BOX
Jazz can generate a low
level forcefield, which is
designed to safeguard his
Spark chamber. However,
he sometimes uses it to
protect his bodywork.

Recessed traction studs

KEEPING UP APPEARANCES

If Jazz has a character flaw, it's that he's
somewhat unwilling to engage in combat in
vehicular mode. He hates the idea of picking
up a dent or scratch to his bodywork, and
would rather transform to robot mode and
go for hand-to-hand combat... or better yet,
just take up a tactical position outside the
main combat zone and call the shots.

FACT BOX
Jazz is always first to put
the pedal to the metal,
utilizing his unique
acceleration feature, which
cuts out several internal
gear processes.

JAZZ

WEAPON MODE

THE BEST DEFENSE...

... is offense. Or at least, that's Jazz's battle credo anyway. That's why his weapon of choice combines elements of both defense and offense in the shape of his custom-built (based on Jazz's own rigorous designs) tri-tanium composite battle shield, with integral cryo-emitter. The rotating shield, laced with tactical sensors that "predict" attacks, is resistant to pretty much anything short of a close range hit from a plasma cannon, and the cryo-emitter fires streams of sub-zero liquid nitrogen, which can freeze an opponent in a matter of seconds. The weapon also has a fast-heat setting, the combination of extreme cold and sudden heat enough to crack the toughest battle armor.

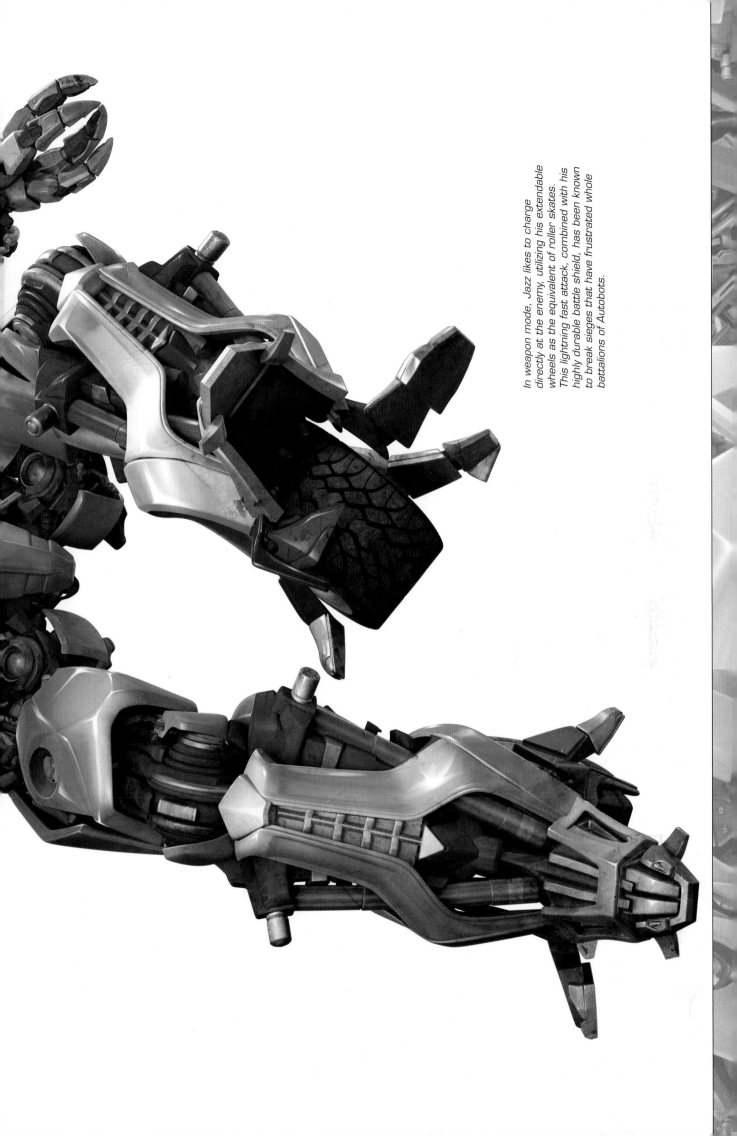

In weapon mode, Jazz likes to charge directly at the enemy, utilizing his extendable wheels as the equivalent of roller skates. This lightning fast attack, combined with his highly durable battle shield, has been known to break sieges that have frustrated whole battalions of Autobots.

"OUR MEDICAL OFFICER, CHIEF EMISSARY TO THE HIGH COUNCIL OF ANCIENTS: RATCHET"

OPTIMUS PRIME

RATCHET

ALTHOUGH HIS OFFICIAL TITLE is Medical Officer, Ratchet is more of an all-around, one-'bot emergency search and rescue specialist. Saving lives is what he does, but actually getting to those in need of treatment is what his particular talents play to. Often, those most in need of his help are in inaccessible or hostile environments, and the tougher and more dangerous the terrain, the more Ratchet likes it. There's nowhere he won't go, no place he fears to tread, and no obstacle he can't overcome.

Vice-grip feature (anti-tremble)

Height: 20' 1"
Weight: 6.7 metric tons
Strength: Power Level 4
Vehicle: Hummer H2

Storage for cutting tools

ALL DUE RESPECT

Though Ratchet functions primarily on the battlefield, he's also at home in the equally thorny realms of diplomacy and negotiation. Before the Great War, Optimus Prime appointed Ratchet his chief liaison to the esteemed High Council of Ancients, Cybertron's equivalent of a senate. With great tact and plenty of due respect, Ratchet was able to heal many a division between state and senate.

FACT BOX
Ratchet is built for strength not speed. His durable, heavy-duty armature ensures he gets where he's going in one piece... but not necessarily at the double.

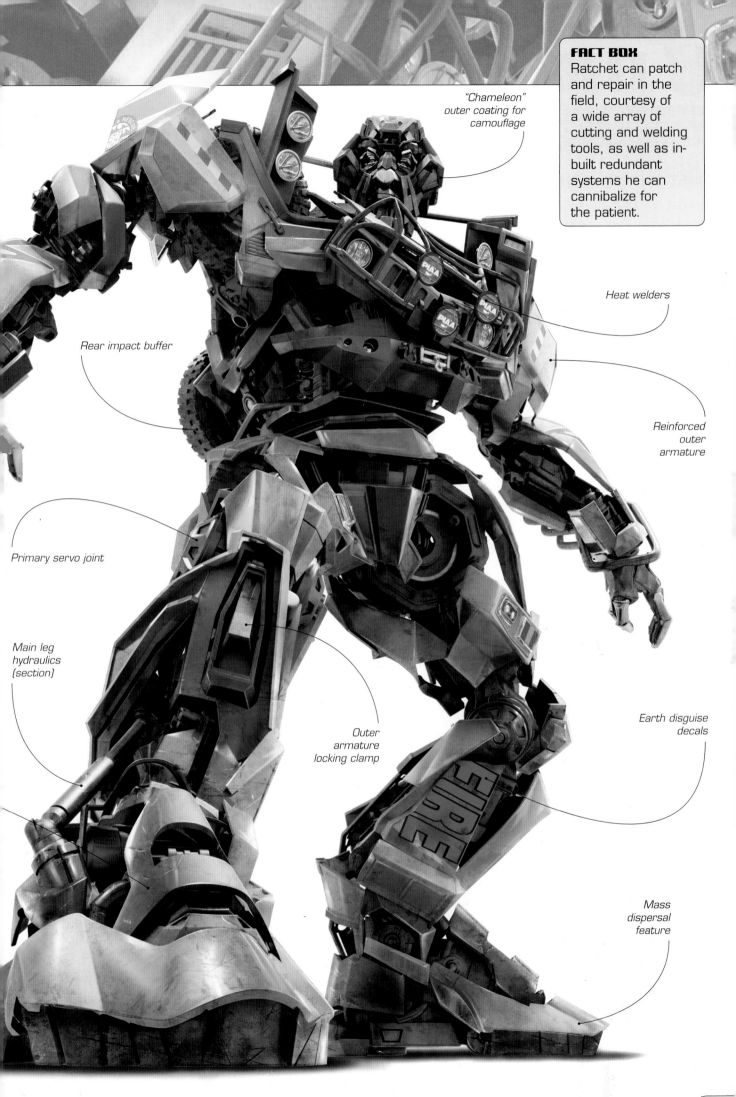

"Chameleon"
outer coating for
camouflage

FACT BOX
Ratchet can patch
and repair in the
field, courtesy of
a wide array of
cutting and welding
tools, as well as in-
built redundant
systems he can
cannibalize for
the patient.

Heat welders

Rear impact buffer

Reinforced
outer
armature

Primary servo joint

Main leg
hydraulics
(section)

Earth disguise
decals

Outer
armature
locking clamp

Mass
dispersal
feature

VEHICLE MODE

RATCHET'S DRAMATIC ARRIVAL ON Earth, right in the heart of Tranquility's downtown district, brought emergency vehicles screaming to the scene. Ratchet had carefully chosen his landing site and equally avoided causing any loss of life in the process. The occupants of one particular Hummer H2 rescue vehicle were oblivious to strange alien rays that mapped and detailed every inch of their vehicle. Moments later, from the site of the crash-landing, an identical Hummer H2 emerged. Ratchet had arrived.

"Daylight" halogen lamps (x4)

Load locking gantry

Charging indicators

Rear load bearing ramp

FACT BOX
Ratchet can haul (or push) 20 times his own (considerable) weight and mass, using a vibrational force distribution system located under his main chassis.

Chameleon detailing

All-terrain tires

Force distribution system (section)

FIRE DEPARTMENT
SEARCH & RESCUE

Top speed: 230mph

0-60 in: 3.65 seconds

Engine: 650 HP

Max haulage: 134 metric tons

FACT BOX

Ratchet's ramming bars are made from a molded silicate/metal amalgam of incredible density, giving him the strength to smash through obstacles.

Emergency signals

Forward ramming bars

THE ONE

Long ago Ratchet told himself (in relation to those who lay dying on the battleground), "You can't save them all." It's a truism that his logic center accepts but his Spark routinely overrules. He could save a hundred lives, a thousand, but it's the one he can't save that haunts him. And when those individuals are Ratchet's allies and close friends, being unable to help them is even harder to bear.

Spectrographic spotlights

Main forward coupling

LIFE AND LIMB

The mistake enemies often make with Ratchet is assuming that because he is sworn to safeguard and protect life and limb he's somehow unwilling to really let loose when in battle. It's not a mistake they get to make twice! Ratchet is more than willing to bring his considerable presence to bear in combat situations, and his strength and durability mean he'll take on anyone... even Megatron!

Vibrational force buffers

RATCHET

WEAPON MODE

UNARMED AND DANGEROUS

Ratchet would tell you, if asked, that he doesn't actually possess a weapon mode. His detachable, bi-directional cutters (forged from a rare super-ore known as tyrrenium) are simply the tools of his trade, used to clear tangled wreckage or cut through otherwise impenetrable metal bulkheads. Ask any Decepticon who's ever gone up against Ratchet in close-combat (and survived) and he'll tell you that those selfsame whirling buzz-saw blades, spinning (one clockwise, one anticlockwise) at up to 400 rpm are a lethal force to be reckoned with and met head on at one's peril.

In "weapon" mode, Ratchet can—in dire circumstances—disengage the restraining cap on the central spindle, allowing the blades to fly off in random directions. Of course, with no real way to predict their scything trajectory, they can just as easily injure him as any Decepticons in the general vicinity.

AUTHOR ACKNOWLEDGMENTS

OF COURSE, THIS BOOK could not have been written without access to the *TRANSFORMERS* movie script, and I am therefore indebted to the stellar work of authors John Rogers, Robert Orci, and Alex Kurtzman. Thanks also to IDW's Chris Ryall, who involved me so greatly in the movie prequel comics, which in turn provided so much of the formative groundwork for the characters and institutions featured in this book. And, as always, thanks to the legions of loyal TRANSFORMERS fans, without whom none of this would have happened at all.

DK WOULD LIKE TO thank Ed Lane, Michael Kelly, and Frances Hinds at Hasbro for their assistance.